Building the Three Gorges Dam

L. Patricia Kite

EXPRESS EDITION

Raintree

Chicago, Illi

www.heinemannraintree.com
Visit our website to find out more information about Heinemann-Raintree books.

To order:
☎ Phone 888-454-2279
🖳 Visit www.heinemannraintree.com to browse our catalog and order online.

Edited by Adam Miller, Andrew Farrow, and
  Adrian Vigliano
Designed by Philippa Jenkins
Original illustrations © Capstone Global Library
  Ltd.
Illustrated by KJA-artists.com
Picture research by Tracy Cummins
Production by Alison Parsons
Originated by Capstone Global Library Ltd
Printed in the United States of America by
  Worzalla Publishing

14 13 12 11 10
10 9 8 7 6 5 4 3 2 1

Library of Congress Cataloging-in-Publication Data
Cataloging-in-Publication data is on file at the Library of Congress.

ISBN: 978-1-4109-3992-0 (HC)
     978-1-4109-3999-9 (PB)

Acknowledgments
The author and publishers are grateful to the following for permission to reproduce copyright material: Alamy ©Eye Ubiquitous **p. 9**; Alamy ©Tina Manley **p. 13**; AP Photo/Xinhua, Du Huaju **pp. 4 & 5**; AP Photo/Xinhua **p. 24**; AP Photo/Xinhua, Zha Chunming **p. 25**; AP Photo/Xinhua, Li Gang **pp. 26 & 27**; AP Images/Imaginechina **p. 29**; AP Photo/Xinhua, Du Huaju **p. 38**; Corbis ©Long Hongtao/Xinhua Press **p. 7**; Corbis ©REUTERS/China Photo **p. 8**; Corbis ©Swim Ink **p. 12**; Corbis ©Huang Wen/China Features/Sygma **pp. 14 & 15**; Corbis ©Diego Azubel/epa **p. 18**; Corbis ©Fritz Hoffmann **pp. 20 & 21**; Corbis ©Bob Sacha **p. 22**; Corbis ©Liu Liqun **p. 28**; Corbis ©Du Huaju/Xinhua Press **p. 32**; Corbis ©Xiaoyang Liu **pp. 34 & 35**; Corbis ©Zheng Jiayu/XinHua/Xinhua Press **p. 39**; Corbis ©Zhai Dong Feng/Redlink **p. 40**; Corbis ©Keren Su **p. 41**; Corbis ©Keren Su **p. 42**; Corbis ©CHINA NEWSPHOTO/Reuters **p. 44**; Getty Images/China Photos **p. 23**; Getty Images/China Photos **pp. 30 & 31**; Getty Images/ZOU QING/AFP **p. 45**; Getty Images/Tim Graham **pp. 46 & 47**; Mary Evans ©Illustrated London News Ltd **pp. 10 & 11**; Shutterstock ©JingAiping **p. 16**; Shutterstock ©claudio zaccherini **p. 37**; shutterstock ©Thomas Barrat **pp. 50 & 51**.

Cover photograph of the Three Gorges Dam reproduced with the permission of Corbis ©Xinhua Press.

The author dedicates this book to Will Brant, a joyous addition to the family.

The publishers would like to thank Daniel Block for his invaluable help in the preparation of this book.

Every effort has been made to contact copyright holders of any material reproduced in this book. Any omissions will be rectified in subsequent printings if notice is given to the publisher.

CONTENTS

Some words are printed in bold, **like this**. You can
find out what they mean by looking in the glossary.
You can also look out for them in the **WORD STORE**
box at the bottom of each page.

THE YANGTZE RIVER AND THREE GORGES

The Three **Gorges Dam** project is one of the most expensive, enormous building projects in history. A dam is a structure that is built across water to control how the water flows. The Three Gorges Dam controls the Yangtze River, in the country of China.

The Three Gorges Dam is also a **hydroelectric** plant. It uses the **energy** (ability to do work) of the moving water to create electricity.

Some people see many benefits from the dam project. They say it will help prevent flooding. It will also provide needed electricity. But others argue that the dam was a huge mistake. They feel it will damage the environment. They also feel it will harm local traditions and ways of life.

This book will look at the history of building this enormous dam. It will also look at the benefits and problems of the project.

First, let's take a look at the area where the dam was created.

Water rushes through the gates of the Three Gorges Dam.

The long river

The Yangtze is one of the world's longest rivers. In fact, the word *Yangtze* means "long river." The only longer rivers in the world are the Nile River in Africa and the Amazon River in South America. The Yangtze begins in a place called Tibet, on an icy **plateau**. A plateau is an area of land that is high up and fairly flat.

From there, the icy waters travel about 6,300 kilometers (3,900 miles) through China. Hundreds of smaller rivers and lakes flow into the enormous Yangtze. At the end of its path, the Yangtze reaches the East China Sea.

People have lived and worked along the Yangtze for thousands of years. Today, about 400 million people live along the river's **banks** (the lands that border the water). Major **industrial** cities are located along the Yangtze's banks. These cities have a lot of factories and businesses that make things to sell. The Yangtze is the most-used path for ships traveling between inland China and Shanghai.

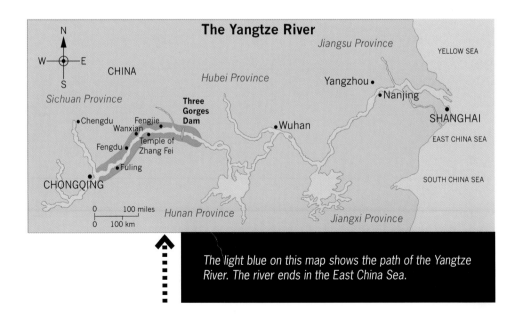

The light blue on this map shows the path of the Yangtze River. The river ends in the East China Sea.

WORD STORE   **bank** land that borders water
dam structure built across water to control water flow

A huge river like the Yangtze can be very different along its path. This section is calm. But other areas of the river can be wild!

Rising water

The Yangtze is calm in some areas. But sometimes it can become very dangerous. With summer heat and wind, snow and ice melt in the Tibetan plateau. This adds a huge amount of water to the river. When it gets moving, this river water can cause flooding.

Before the Three **Gorges Dam** was built, the river water would rise a little in areas with wide banks. But it also had to pass through the narrow mountain area called the Three Gorges. Here, water had to travel through a very small space with tall cliffs. Some of the spaces were so narrow and tall that sunlight never reached the river water.

WORD STORE   **industrial** relating to businesses that make goods
plateau area of land that is high up and fairly flat

The Three Gorges

A **gorge** is a deep, narrow passageway. It has steep, rocky sides that are enclosed between two mountains. This is how the Three Gorges mountain area got its name. It has three gorges. The Three Gorges on the Yangtze River are named Qutang, Wu, and Xiling.

Qutang

The shortest gorge area is Qutang Gorge. It is also the narrowest gorge. Qutang Gorge once contained many **relics**. These objects were left behind from people long ago. Boat-shaped cedar coffins from 1,600 years ago were discovered there. But only a few remained after the Three Gorges **Dam** was built. Other important ancient sites were later covered by rising waters caused by the dam project.

Ancient wooden coffins like these existed along the Yangtze River. Many of these areas are now underwater because of the dam project.

WORD STORE   gorge deep, narrow passageway between two mountains

Wu

The city of Wushan is at the entrance to Wu Gorge. Wu Gorge is noted for its 12 peaks, or points. These peaks are thought to look like animals and people. One famous peak is called the Goddess Peak. It is a beautiful pillar of white stone that looks like a standing maiden.

Xiling

The last of the three gorges is Xiling Gorge. It is the longest and deepest gorge. The cliffs around Xiling Gorge rise to 1,219 meters (4,000 feet) high.

This shows a peak at Wu Gorge.

Xiling Gorge was once considered the most dangerous gorge for boats to pass through. Before the dam project, Three Gorges floodwaters could rise 18 meters (60 feet) in a single day. If the rain continued, water could rise as much as 40 meters (130 feet) higher. When this happened, the water was not only higher. It also became a lot rougher. The Three Gorges area had fast-moving, dangerous waters. There were also rock falls.

WORD STORE   **relic** remains of an object from an earlier time

This market near the Yangtze flooded in 1931.

WHY BUILD A DAM ACROSS THE YANGTZE RIVER?

But why build a **dam** across the Yangtze River? The Chinese leader Sun Yat-sen proposed building the Three **Gorges** Dam back in 1919. He believed that the dam would help improve the Chinese **economy**. An economy is a system in which things are made, bought, and sold. Sun Yat-sen argued that the dam would help ships get through the river more easily. This would help transport goods to be bought and sold. The dam would also create **hydroelectric** power. This could help power factories and businesses. But the dam was not built at that time.

Later, in 1931, **dikes** holding back the river failed. A dike is a raised barrier built to prevent flooding. There were summer floods along the Yangtze that caused the deaths of 145,000 people. People and animals were swept downstream by raging waters. They were buried under mudslides.

Two million homes were swept into the swirling waters. Huge amounts of farmland were washed away. People starved without farm crops or farm animals. They had no shelter or clean water. Often-deadly diseases such as cholera and typhus were also spread by the floodwaters.

More floods

In 1935 there was another major flood along the Yangtze River. It was caused by melting icy waters and heavy rains. This time 142,000 people died. Even more land was flooded.

In 1954 a series of Yangtze River floods caused the deaths of about 33,000 people.

Reasons for a dam

The disasters caused by these floods made leaders in China think. They saw the benefits of building a huge **dam**. In the 1950s, Mao Zedong and other leaders supported building a dam by the Three **Gorges** mountain area. There were four important reasons for building a dam.

敬祝我们伟大的领袖毛主席万寿无疆!

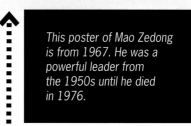

This poster of Mao Zedong is from 1967. He was a powerful leader from the 1950s until he died in 1976.

1. Flood control

Flooding had to be controlled. The Chinese knew that a major Yangtze River flood would occur at least once every 10 years.

2. Shipping

A safe shipping route was desperately needed. Ships traveling between the cities of Chongqing and Shanghai needed a good path. A dam would help provide this path.

WORD STORE **economy** system in which things are made, bought, and sold

3. Replacing coal

A substitute for coal had to be found. Coal was burned for fuel in everything from factory boilers to home stoves. But there were often coal shortages. Burning coal also created air **pollution**. It dirtied the air and made people sick. A new, cleaner fuel was desperately needed.

4. Creating hydroelectric power

Hydroelectric power would be a good, clean substitute for coal. It would also help China's **economy** grow. Before the dam was built, many cities and countryside areas had power shortages. This prevented businesses and factories from producing as much as they could. If people had a new power source, leaders hoped that more business could be done.

This shows the Chinese city of Chongqing. Many cities with factories like this have had problems with poor air quality.

This shows the Gezhouba Dam in 1997.

14

PLANNING THE THREE GORGES DAM

In December 1970, construction began on a **dam** on the Yangtze River. This was the Gezhouba Dam.

At first, people hoped the Gezhouba Dam would make a larger dam near the Three **Gorges** area unnecessary. But there were many problems building the Gezhouba Dam.

After 18 years, the Gezhouba Dam was completed in 1988. At that time, it was the largest dam in China. It is 70 meters (230 feet) high and 2.6 kilometers (1.6 miles) wide.

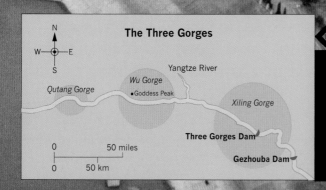

The Three Gorges

N
W — E
S

Yangtze River

Qutang Gorge

Wu Gorge
• Goddess Peak

Xiling Gorge

Three Gorges Dam

Gezhouba Dam

0   50 miles
0   50 km

This map shows the location of the Three Gorges Dam and the Gezhouba Dam. They are in the Three Gorges area, along the Yangtze River.

Arguments and delays

Not everyone agreed that another **dam** was necessary. Many people worried that the Three **Gorges** Dam would be too expensive. They also felt the money could be better spent elsewhere. For example, it could be spent on education and health services. But some Chinese leaders felt the project would prove China's power to the world. They were also eager to get **hydroelectric** power into China.

A final design was due in 1980. But plans for the Three Gorges Dam were delayed. Finally, in 1983 the Chinese government approved plans for a dam. Workers quickly started getting ready to build the dam. Roads and power-supply facilities were also built. The dam would be 170 meters (491 feet) tall.

However, just a year later, some **engineers** (building planners) had concerns. They thought the dam's size would cause major problems for the large city of Chongqing. It would cause **sedimentation** problems (see the box on page 17). Plans were changed to make the dam slightly higher. Supporters of the dam argued that this would make the dam more effective. It would help to prevent floods, cause less sedimentation, and create more power.

After looking at 16 locations, the town of Sandouping was chosen as the location for the Three Gorges Dam. This location along the Yangtze River had many advantages. It had a rock base. This would form a good foundation for the dam. Also, earthquakes in that area were not strong and did not occur often.

WORD STORE   engineer person who designs the structure of a project, such as a dam, and makes sure it will work

The Yangtze River constantly removes and carries material like soil from the surrounding land. This material is called **silt**. Sometimes the Yangtze carries up to 500 million tons of silt a year. Eventually the silt drops to the bottom of the river. This is known as **sediment**. Over 700 million tons of sediment is deposited every year into the Yangtze River.

Over time, more and more of this sediment collects. This process is called sedimentation. Sedimentation is a danger to structures like dams. This is because this thick, gooey layer can clog things like gates. It can also cause flooding (see pages 24 and 25) and dirty water (see the photo below).

This image of the Yangtze near Chongqing shows high levels of sedimentation. This is why the water appears brown.

Areas of rich farmland along the Yangtze River like this were flooded. They became part of the Three Gorges Dam reservoir.

WORD STORE   **reservoir** place where water is collected and stored for use

Concerns and approval

Many people in China started to question the Three **Gorges Dam**. China's leaders continued to disagree about the details of the plan. One problem was that at least 1.3 million people had to move. These people lived in areas that would be flooded by the new dam **reservoir**. A reservoir is a place where water is collected and stored for use.

New businesses were created to provide jobs for relocated people. A few of these businesses eventually succeeded. Other projects were failures, though. (See pages 46 to 49 for more about relocation.)

In 1986 an important organization said it did not support the construction of the Three Gorges Dam. Among its concerns were how to control floods and how to reduce **sedimentation** problems (see page 17).

But in 1989 a group from the country of Canada said that the Three Gorges Dam was a good idea. Now it looked like the Chinese government would go ahead with plans to build the dam. But only a few months later, the government vote was delayed.

By 1990 Chinese leader Li Peng created a group to review the Three Gorges project once again. In 1992 a plan for a 185-meter (607-foot) dam received the go-ahead. But many members of the government did not offer their support. The dam project would never be popular with everyone.

CONSTRUCTION

At last, construction could begin on the Three **Gorges Dam**. But tons of materials and thousands of workers needed to get to the mountainous dam location.

A new four-lane highway, the Three Gorges Project Expressway, was cut through the mountains. Along this expressway there would be 34 bridges and 5 double-lane tunnels. In addition, the Xiling Yangtze Bridge was built at Sandouping. This provided access to the right side of the dam.

STAGE ONE

In 1994 the first stage of work began. A dam could not be built until the Yangtze River had been **diverted**. Diverting something means creating a new path for it. Workers created a **diversion channel** for the waters. This was an area where the water could be moved during construction. They used dump trucks and giant drills that cut through granite (a rock).

In November 1997, thousands of loading trucks poured tons of rock and gravel. This created a wall closing in the dam. When the river moved into the diversion channel, fireworks went off. Ships' horns blared. Thousands of people cheered.

A local woman stands above the Three Gorges Dam during construction.

Cofferdams

As the workers built the **dam**, they needed a dry area for their work. So, huge **cofferdams** were built. Cofferdams are temporary, watertight walls used in underwater construction projects. The water is pumped out of the walled areas.

Forced out

As construction began, thousands of local people had to leave their homes. By 1995 the area was filled with steel and iron bridges and concrete walls. There were huge holes in the ground and piles of dirt. Red and yellow bulldozers moved back and forth.

A worker stands beside one of the Three Gorges cofferdams.

WORD STORE **cofferdam** temporary, watertight wall used in underwater construction projects

The tiny town of Dachang dated back 1,700 years. It had changed very little over its history. There were ancient city gates, stone roads, and houses.

But Dachang was in the path of the flooding that would create the Three **Gorges reservoir.** In 2003 the Chinese government decided to save at least some of Dachang. Thirty-eight houses were saved. Workers carefully took apart the buildings, brought them to a new, safer site, and rebuilt them.

The photo below shows a part of Dachang that was not moved. It was eventually destroyed by the reservoir.

Another flood

In 1998 there was a huge flood along the Yangtze River. Five million houses were destroyed. Huge areas of farmland went underwater. Thirteen million people had to be moved. At least 1,000 people died. The difficulties that resulted delayed some of the **dam** construction.

During the 1998 Yangtze flooding, many people built boats to go about their daily lives.

STAGE TWO

From 1998 to 2003, stage two of the project was finished. More **cofferdams** were constructed. Many important projects were completed. For example, workers completed the electricity station.

WORD STORE   capacity total amount that something can contain

As the dam walls grew higher, the blocked waters behind the walls rose about 5 meters (16 feet) per day. To save money, project officials wanted the **reservoir** filled more quickly.

But experts worried about filling up the reservoir too quickly. **Sedimentation** could possibly block the dam's **sluice** gates. Sluice gates are paths with gates that control the flow of water. If these gates became blocked, the whole dam could fail. The water would no longer be controlled. (See page 5 for a photo of the sluice gates.)

Buildup of mud and soil behind the dam and throughout the reservoir would take up room. This would affect the overall reservoir storage **capacity**. The capacity is how much water the dam can hold. With less storage capacity, the dam would be able to hold—and control—less floodwater.

But construction continued. By 2003 the blocked waters in the reservoir rose to the second-stage goal of 156 meters (511 feet). The dam could now start to create electricity.

A building is blown up to make way for the reservoir.

WORD STORE   **sluice** human-made channel for directing water. It uses a valve or gate to control the flow.

THE
LOCK SYSTEM

As **dam** construction continued, large ships had a problem. As the ships traveled on the Yangtze River, how would they get past the high Three **Gorges** Dam? The Chinese **economy** depended on having these ships transport lots of goods.

Eventually a two-lane **lock** system was designed. A lock system is like a huge series of elevators. They move boats using water levels. The lock system's purpose is to get ships from one side of the dam to the other. Ships must be moved 113 meters (370 feet) down to get from the **reservoir** side of the dam to the river. But the lock system can move ships up as well as down.

Space had to be created for the five lock chambers. So, workers blasted enormous amounts of granite from the sides of the Yangtze River.

To the right, you can see a large ship leaving the bottom lock chamber. Above it you can see the five chambers the ship lowered through.

Locks and lifts

A ship entering a **lock** would be moved up, or down, in a series of five steps. This would be enough to carry it across the **dam**. A large ship might take about three to four hours to get through.

Construction of the lock took nine years. It began to be used in 2003. It cost almost $747 million. The lock system is the largest in the world.

Not all ships crossing the new dam are enormous. So, a smaller ship lift was built just for smaller business or tourist ships. It was completed in 2009. These ships are taken directly up to the river in one step. It takes about 40 minutes to be lifted.

To meet deadlines, thousands of workers had to pour concrete at a fast pace. This required a complex system for moving concrete from the mixing plants to the dam.

Constructing the lock system was another huge piece of the dam project.

WORD STORE   **lock** system similar to an enormous elevator that works in steps. Locks move boats up or down in a body of water.

RELOCATING AN ANCIENT TEMPLE

The Zhang Fei Temple was in the **reservoir's** path. To protect it from disappearing, experts began work to move it.

The Zhang Fei Temple dates back about 1,700 years. Zhang Fei was a brave and loyal warrior. This beautiful temple was dedicated to him. Inside the temple were more than 600 beautiful sculptures and woodcarvings.

Experts took apart the ancient temple piece by piece. Every part was numbered, wrapped in cloth, and loaded onto trucks. The team also carefully moved plants, railings, rocks, and stone stairs.

The trucks transferred the items to a gigantic boat. The boat took the pieces of the temple to a new location in Bangshang Yuanzi. It was then rebuilt.

This is the Zhang Fei Temple after it was moved and rebuilt.

GENERATING POWER

Various problems developed as the **dam** was built. Large cracks in the dam's concrete had to be fixed. The repairs cost a lot of money. But then inspectors found that some of the repaired cracks had reopened. There were also several accidents, including a bridge collapse. Some people said that the group paid to do the work used equipment and materials that were too cheap.

The Chinese government demanded that some parts of the dam should be destroyed and rebuilt.

By the end of stage three (2004–2009), the dam's water level had risen to its goal. It was 175 meters (574 feet) tall. The **reservoir** was capable of storing 19 trillion liters (5 trillion gallons) of water. It was ready to create full **hydroelectric** power.

The **cofferdams** were no longer needed. The last cofferdam was blown up in June 2006. Removing the cofferdams meant the dam could now create electricity.

葛洲坝集 CGGC 围堰爆破圆满成功

This shows the explosion caused by a cofferdam being blown up in 2006.

A lot of power

During this final construction stage, the power station on the left **bank** of the **dam** began working. The permanent ship **lock** system was available for use. The dam sections and power station on the right bank of the dam were completed.

On October 30, 2008, the 26th **generator** was brought into action. Generators are large electric motors. They help turn water power into electricity (see the box on page 33). This meant that all of the planned project parts were completed. The goal was to supply 10 percent of China's electricity needs.

The completed Three **Gorges** Dam project will contain 32 main generators. The six additional generators in the underground power plant will not be fully in use until 2011.

This photo was taken Inside one of the power stations on the dam's right bank.

WORD STORE **generator** large electric motor
hydroelectric electric current produced by moving water

HYDROELECTRIC POWER

Hydroelectric power is produced as water moves through a dam and into the river below. Inside the powerhouse, generators are connected on top of **turbines**. Turbines are propeller-like machines. The power of moving water causes them to turn. As water turns a turbine, the parts of a generator turn, too. This produces electricity.

All kinds of electricity are usually produced by turning turbines. Nuclear and coal power plants create heat to make steam. Steam turns turbines. Dams use the natural movement of a river to turn turbines.

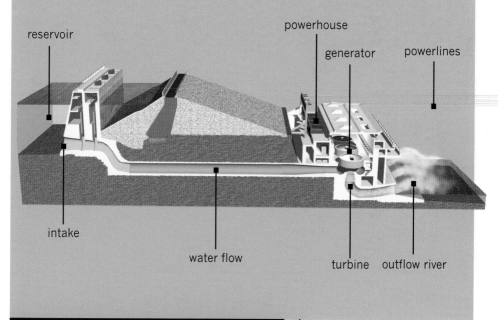

reservoir

powerhouse

generator

powerlines

intake

water flow

turbine   outflow river

This diagram shows how a dam like Three Gorges produces power. The natural movement of the river water is used to turn turbines. These produce electricity with each rotation.

The Three Gorges Dam project has both benefits and problems.

BENEFITS
AND
PROBLEMS

Supporters of the Three **Gorges Dam** believe that the project's benefits make up for any problems. But other people disagree. Let's begin by taking a look at the project's benefits.

The dam was designed to prevent the flooding that occurred along the Yangtze River about every 10 years. Millions of people live downstream from the dam. Many large, important cities are next to the river.

If a major flood occurs, the dam is expected to make the flooding effects less harmful. The dam's **reservoir** is expected to reduce the flooding of the Yangtze by 90 percent.

How will it do this? The water level in the reservoir can be adjusted. As the rainy season approaches, additional storage **capacity** is needed. To achieve this, the reservoir water can be lowered to the flood-control level of 145 meters (476 feet) high. This allows the reservoir to accept and store more water.

Incoming water will cause the **reservoir** to reach its maximum height. Then, the water will be released in a safe, controlled way. This idea was tested when a large rainfall occurred in 2009. The **dam** succeeded in controlling the raging waters.

The dam can also help when there is a **drought** (too little water because of low rainfall). During a drought, water flows can be increased.

Generating power

As we have seen, China is developing new businesses and factories. As a result, it needs lots of **energy**. The **hydroelectric** power created by the Three **Gorges** Dam is enormous. In fact, the Three Gorges Dam is the biggest hydroelectric producer in the world. Its output should produce about 10 percent of China's electricity needs. Supporters hope that the dam will play an important role in the further growth of China's **economy**.

Reducing pollution

If people use hydroelectric power, they will not need to use as much coal for energy. By not using coal, this reduces air **pollution**. Coal power plants release many harmful gases into the air. They also release dust and other discharge into the air.

Providing freshwater

The Three Gorges Dam also provides a lot of freshwater to downstream cities and farms during the dry season. This has helped to ease some of the effects of drought.

WORD STORE   **drought** shortage of water caused by unusually low rainfall

Chinese cities like Shanghai show how much China's economy has grown. But huge power demands have come along with this growth.

Improving navigation

The Three **Gorges Dam** and **reservoir** make it easier to travel on the Yangtze River. Now there is a clear pathway of calm, deep water. The shipping lanes are wider.

The Three Gorges Dam allows heavy ships to travel on the river. These ships carry goods for businesses.

Creating new forests

There are forests along the Yangtze River. As China's **population** (number of people) increased, many forests were cut down to make room for homes. Trees were also cut down and used to build homes. As more factories opened, they used more wood products like furniture and paper.

Within the last 50 years, over 50 percent of local forests have disappeared. As trees were removed, so were their roots. These deep root systems helped make the land stable. Without these roots, **landslides** have occurred. This means that land suddenly falls down a slope. Landslides have destroyed villages and valuable farmland. The Chinese government has proposed a plan to replant forests within the Three Gorges area.

A local man fishes below the dam. Debate continues about how the dam will affect people's lives.

WORD STORE   landslide when land suddenly falls down a slope

Cleaning wastewater

In 2001, $2.55 billion was spent on cleanup projects. Factories causing too much **pollution** have been closed or required to change. In 2001 a special site was created to clean wastewater. By 2007 about 65 percent of the Yangtze wastewater was treated before being dumped in the Three Gorges Dam reservoir. Currently about 18 wastewater treatment sites have been constructed. Also, 101 more are planned in the countryside.

*Large ships pass through the Three Gorges **lock** system.*

WORD STORE   **population** number of people living in an area

More improvements

Supporters argue that the raising and lowering of the **reservoir** water should control the bits of mud and soil that collect in the water. When the water level is high, these bits will be flushed out. Experts are developing new ways to address worries about **sedimentation** (see page 17).

Yichang, the nearest city to the Three **Gorges Dam**, has added four new trains. These link the city with the major cities of Shanghai and Guangzhou. There is a new international airport based in Yichang. Supporters of the dam argue that these improvements would not have happened without it.

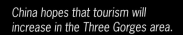

China hopes that tourism will increase in the Three Gorges area.

"White Crane Ridge," or Baiheliang, is a huge stone ridge. It is engraved with carvings about the Yangtze River. These date from 763 to the early 1900s. On the huge rock are 20 fish sculptures that serve as water-level markers. The ridge went underwater when it became part of the dam's reservoir. An underwater museum was built so that people can still admire this work of art.

This photo shows a section of White Crane Ridge before it was covered by water.

Now that the dam is complete, Three Gorges tourism is an increasingly big business. People come to see the dam. They also visit the Yangtze River and the changed Three Gorges Mountain area.

Dam supporters say that important places and objects from history located in the dam area are protected better than ever before.

They also argue that the dam will bring jobs and an improved quality of life to tens of millions of people. But it remains to be seen if this is true.

Criticisms

From the beginning, many people have spoken out about possible problems with the Three **Gorges Dam** project. Some of these concerns have been proven correct.

The reservoir caused towns like this to go completely underwater.

Destruction and flooding

Thirteen major cities, 140 small cities and towns, and 1,352 villages were flooded by the **reservoir**. So were 1,600 factories and 700 schools. Many have totally disappeared.

Some people believe that the dam's flood-control benefits are not very great. They argue that the new reservoir can store only a small part of the floodwaters entering the Yangtze River.

Pollution

Over one billion tons of wastewater go into the Yangtze River every year. As this dirty water travels downstream toward the dam, it collects more waste. Chongqing and many other cities along the river put huge amounts of poisonous waste into the reservoir. The dam has slowed the Yangtze flow. This reduces its ability to flush out waste. There is now more waste than the water can clean by itself.

In 2008 the State Environmental Policy Protection Administration of China stated that the water quality behind the Three Gorges Dam has not improved much. Plans to reduce **pollution** have not worked well. Water quality is actually getting worse in several parts of the Yangtze.

Two-thirds of the dam's promised environmental projects are not yet in place. Some 460 water-quality projects are set to begin during the next few years. These water programs will help, but only if completed and watched closely.

Power problems

There is not enough electricity coming from the dam. China's power needs grow as businesses expand and new cities are built. The dam was supposed to supply 10 percent of China's electricity. But it may only produce 3 percent.

Silting and sedimentation

Critics think bits of mud and soil will collect behind the **dam** walls. The **turbines** will clog. This would reduce the dam's effectiveness in flood control.

People also worry that the river will not flow fast enough to keep the turbines turning. The dam might become unable to operate. If the buildup of mud and soil becomes thick enough, it might even cause the **reservoir** water to create a major waterfall. This would happen if water rose above the dam wall.

Earthquakes and landslides

The Three **Gorges** Dam lies over a **fault** line. A fault is crack in Earth's crust (surface) where earthquakes often strike. The dam is supposed to be able to hold up against earthquakes. But the reservoir area also sees frequent mudslides and **landslides**.

Underwater earthquakes and landslides can move huge amounts of water. Huge waves of water could fall over the dam's top.

Chinese sturgeon have suffered because of the new dam.

Endangered animals

The Yangtze River is home to many animals that live in the water. The Three Gorges Dam has increased river traffic. This has led to **pollution** and the loss of many animal's natural homes.

WORD STORE   **fault** crack in Earth's surface (crust) where earthquakes often strike

Animals that live in water have not been able to deal with the huge changes to the river. About 80 different kinds of fish are in danger of dying out. So are the finless porpoise, Chinese alligator, and Siberian crane.

Cultural loss

During the construction of the dam, about 1,300 building sites were flooded. Some historic objects and buildings were moved. But others could not be moved due to their location, size, or design.

This photo shows Fengdu before the dam was completed. Fengdu is an important place for people who follow the Buddhist religion. After the reservoir filled, the water level rose as high as the bridge.

POPULATION MOVEMENT

In 1990 the costs for the Three **Gorges Dam** were guessed to be at $12 billion. It is believed that the final cost will reach $50 billion. This is more than any other single construction cost in history. However, about half of the costs have been from relocating people.

An estimated 1.3 million people, perhaps as many as 2 million, were moved from the Three Gorges area as the dam was built. Their hometowns needed to be destroyed to make way for the dam project. This cut them off from their history and homes.

The Chinese government built 13 new towns. The new cities offered new buildings and apartment houses. They all had modern features like indoor bathrooms. These new homes were more expensive than the homes they had left behind.

Relocating millions of people is a very difficult problem. It also raises many important questions.

This is one of many new towns built to house people relocated from the Three Gorges *reservoir* area.

Struggling to adjust

Many people in Yangtze are still struggling to adjust to the changes brought about by the **dam**. Some newcomers opened small shops so that people could purchase items for their new homes. The new stores contained washing machines, flooring, wallpapers, curtains, and furniture. There was even advice offered on how to make a new home look pretty. There are new drugstores, hairdressers, restaurants, and tailors. Young people have adjusted especially well. They have been pleased that the new schools have better equipment than their previous ones.

But the situation has been more difficult for the 400,000 people who were relocated from the countryside. Many families had been in their villages for many years. People married from their village or from a nearby village.

Years of hard work had improved these people's land. The land could grow fruits, grains, and vegetables. This fed families and provided people with enough money to live on. But the **reservoir** flooded some of the best farmland in the region. Resettled people who continued farming had to do so on poorer-quality land. Some people were moved to lands that were not good for growing anything at all.

The Chinese government knew it would be difficult to transfer poor farmers. But the transfer proved more difficult than they had expected. It was even more difficult for those who were transferred far from their original homes.

WORD STORE   **dialect** version of a language that is unique to a specific group of people or area

Some farmers volunteered to be transferred far away from the Three **Gorges** area. They hoped for a better situation. But they found different farming methods that they did not understand. They also found neighbors who spoke a different **dialect** (version of Chinese) that they did not understand. Almost all of these volunteers asked to be relocated closer to their original homes.

Success or failure?

The Three Gorges Dam project is an amazing example of technology. The dam arose with the pressure of having the world watching at every step. The dam works. But does it work as expected? That depends on who offers an opinion. There is no easy answer when dealing with science and human activity on such a huge scale. Only time will tell if the project was a major success or a disastrous failure.

THREE GORGES DAM STATISTICS

The Three Gorges Dam wall is 185 meters (610 feet) high. That is as high as a 60-story building. It stretches 2.3 kilometers (1.4 miles) across the Yangtze River. The project required 463 tons of steel—enough to build 63 Eiffel Towers. It used 10.5 billion tons of cement.

About 60,000 workers were employed by the Three Gorges Dam project. During construction, about 100 workers died in accidents.

TIMELINE OF THE THREE GORGES DAM PROJECT

1919 Sun Yat-sen proposes a flood-control **dam** for the Three **Gorges** area. The dam idea does not progress.

1931 The Yangtze River causes a major flood.

1935 The Yangtze River causes another major flood.

1953 Chinese leader Mao Zedong proposes a flood-control dam for the Three Gorges area.

1954 The Yangtze River causes another major flood.

1970 The Gezhouba Dam is proposed instead of the Three Gorges Dam.

1988 The Gezhouba Dam is completed, but is not a satisfactory substitute for the Three Gorges Dam.

1990 Leader Li Peng insists on a review of the Three Gorges Dam project.

1992 The Chinese government votes in favor of the Three Gorges Dam project.

1993 Construction teams enter the dam site for the first time.

1993–1997 Stage one of construction gets underway on the Three Gorges Dam. This includes moving earth and the completion of **cofferdams**. The Yangtze River is dammed and construction of the ship lift is completed. The **diversion channel** opens, and ships begin traveling through it. The expressway from Yichang to the dam site, and Xiling Bridge across the Yangtze, are open to traffic.

1998 The Yangtze River causes another major flood.

1998–2003 Stage two of construction gets underway. This includes the completion of the dam's spillway and left **bank** powerhouse. There is continued construction of the permanent ship **lock** system. The first two **turbine generators** begin producing power.

2003–2008 All 26 electricity-producing turbines are completed. The last cofferdam is destroyed. The ship lock begins full operation. **Reservoir** water depth is 175 meters (574 feet).

GLOSSARY

bank land that borders water

capacity total amount that something can contain

cofferdam temporary, watertight wall used in underwater construction projects

dam structure built across water to control water flow

dialect version of a language that is unique to a specific group of people or area. In a large country like China, there are different Chinese dialects in different parts of the country.

dike raised barrier built to prevent or control flooding

diversion channel area where water is redirected while a dam is built

divert create a new path for something

drought shortage of water caused by unusually low rainfall

economy system in which things are made, bought, and sold

energy ability to do work

engineer person who designs the structure of a project, such as a dam, and makes sure it will work

fault crack in Earth's crust (surface) where earthquakes often strike

generator very large electric motor. Generators are used to create electricity.

gorge deep, narrow passageway. It has steep, rocky sides that are enclosed between two mountains.

hydroelectric electric current produced by the energy of moving water

industrial having to do with businesses that process raw materials and make goods in factories

landslide when land suddenly slides down a slope

lock system similar to an enormous elevator that works in steps. Locks are used to move boats up or down in a body of water.

plateau area of land that is high up and fairly flat

pollution human-made waste that dirties something like the air or water

population number of people living in an area

relic remains of an object from an earlier time

reservoir place where water is collected and stored for use

sediment small bits of mud and soil that drop to the bottom of water

sedimentation process in which sediment collects

silt tiny bits of mud or fine soil in moving water

sluice human-made channel for directing water. It uses a valve or gate to control the flow.

turbine piece of a dam that moves to turn a generator

FIND OUT MORE

BOOKS

Barter, James. *The Yangtze*. San Diego: Lucent, 2003.

Behnke, Alison. *China in Pictures*. Minneapolis: Lerner, 2003.

Bowden, Rob. *The Yangtze*. Chicago: Raintree, 2004.

Hansen, Amy S. *Hydropower: Making a Splash!* New York: PowerKids, 2010.

Petersen, Christine. *Water Power*. New York: Children's Press, 2004.

Sebag-Montefiore, Poppy. *Modern China* (*Eyewitness* series). New York: Dorling Kindersley, 2007.

Streissguth, Thomas. *China in the 21st Century: A New World Power*. Berkeley Heights, N.J.: Enslow, 2008.

WEBSITES

Water Use: Hydroelectric Power
http://ga.water.usgs.gov/edu/wuhy.html
This site has a discussion of hydroelectric worldwide. It looks at the good and bad points of hydroelectric power.

Hydroelectric Power: How It Works
http://ga.water.usgs.gov/edu/hyhowworks.html
This site discusses how we get electricity from water.

TVA Kids: Hydroelectric Power
www.tvakids.com/electricity/hydro.htm
This site has more in-depth discussions of hydroelectric power. It also has information about other kinds of power.

Great Wall Across the Yangtze: Three Gorges Dam
www.pbs.org/itvs/greatwall/dam.html
This site has a discussion of the dam's history. It also discusses the dam's good and bad points.

Exploring Chinese History: Special Report: The Three Gorges Dam Project
www.ibiblio.org/chinesehistory/contents/07spe/ specrep01.html
This site has an article that examines some of the major effects of the dam.

TOPICS TO LEARN MORE ABOUT

- **The Communist Party of China**
  Research the Chinese system of government and find out how projects like the Three Gorges Dam are dealt with.

- **Hydroelectric power and other renewable energy sources**
  Is hydroelectric power the best option for countries as they try to move away from "dirty" energy sources like coal? Research other "clean" energy options, such as solar (Sun) power and wind power, to see what the good and bad points are for each.

INDEX